COLOR AND LIGHT

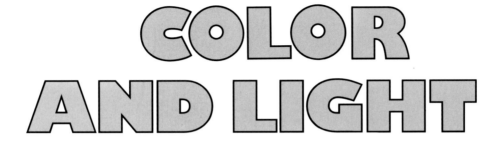

Barbara Taylor

Photographs by Peter Millard

FRANKLIN WATTS
New York • London • Sydney • Toronto

Design: Janet Watson

Science consultant: Dr Bryson Gore

Educational consultants: Kay Davies and
Wendy Oldfield

Series editor: Debbie Fox

The author and publisher would like to thank the
following children for their participation in the
photography of this book: Faiza Ahmed, Kemi
Benjamin, Kate Jones and Christakis Phillipou of
Bands Green Junior School. We are also grateful to
Julia Edwards (Head teacher) and Sue Irvine
(teacher).

Franklin Watts Inc.
387 Park Avenue South
New York, NY 10016

Library of Congress Cataloging in Publication Data:

Taylor, Barbara, 1954-
    Color and light / by Barbara Taylor.
        p. cm. – (Science starters)
    Includes index
    Summary: Explains the properties of light which make
    variation in color possible and suggests projects and
    experiments to demonstrate such principles.
    ISBN 0-531-14015-6
    1. Color – Juvenile literature. 2. Color – Experiments
    – Juvenile literature. 3. Light – Juvenile literature. 4. Light –
    Experiments – Juvenile literature. [I. Color – Experiments.
    2. Light – Experiments. 3. Experiments.] I. Title. II. Series.
    QC495.5.T38 1990
    535.6 – dc20   89-16686
                                                         CIP
                                                          AC

Printed in Belgium

CONTENTS

This book is all about the rainbow colors
in white light, how we see colored light
and how we use colors. It is divided into
five sections. Each has a different
colored triangle at the corner of the
page. Use these triangles to help you find
the different sections.

These red triangles at the corner of the
tinted panels show you where a step-by-
step investigation starts.

Color messages   4
How we use colors to pass on
information; a world without color

Camouflage and danger   6
Animal camouflage and
warning colors

Rainbow colors   8
The spectrum of colors in white
light; rainbows; colors in laser light

Seeing colors   12
Colors and our eyes; painting colors;
background colors; color blindness;
printing colors

Creeping colors   18
Separating colors; chromatography

Changing color   20
Stained glass windows; color filters

Colored light   22
Mixing colored lights;
lighting effects

Sky colors   24
Why the sky is blue; sunrise and
sunset colors

Bubbles, shells and puddles   26
Colors caused by interference

More things to do   28

Did you know?   30

Glossary   31

Index   32

COLOR MESSAGES

When you are watching a soccer match, how do you tell one team from the other?

Each team wears different colors so it is easy to tell them apart. We use colors to pass on messages about all kinds of things. Think about the way colors are used in traffic lights, on flags, on television and on posters and advertisements.

What would the world look like if you could not see colors? You would have much less information about your surroundings. Can you guess what these children are drinking? Have they all got the same drink?

With a color picture, you can easily see that each child has a different drink. What color is your favorite drink?

We can see lots of different colors, but many animals cannot see the colors we see. Cats, dogs, horses and cows see the world in shades of black, white and gray. They rely more on their other senses, such as smell and hearing.

Reptiles (like snakes and lizards), birds, butterflies, bees and many fishes can see in color.

CAMOUFLAGE...

The skins of many animals, like this chameleon, are dull colors that match their surroundings. These colors help to camouflage the animals and make it hard for enemies to see them. A chameleon is especially good at camouflage, because it can change the color of its skin very quickly to match its surroundings. Can you find out the names of any other animals that can change the color of their skin?

Birdwatchers wear camouflage colors to help them get closer to wild birds without disturbing them. If birds see people coming, they soon fly away.

...AND DANGER

This frog doesn't need to hide. Its bright colors warn other animals that it is very poisonous. So they leave it alone.

We use bright warning colors in safety clothes and on emergency vehicles such as fire engines, police cars and ambulances. If you go walking in the mountains, it is a good idea to wear brightly colored clothes. Do you know why?

If you lose your way or someone becomes ill, rescue teams will be able to find you more easily if your clothes stand out against the green and brown countryside.

RAINBOW COLORS

How many colors can you see in this rainbow? Do you know where the colors come from?

Sunlight or electric light looks white. But it is really made up of lots of colors – we can usually see red, orange, yellow, green, blue, indigo and violet. These colors are called a spectrum, which means "ghost." A rainbow is a spectrum in the sky. It appears like magic when the sun shines through the rain. This is because the raindrops make the colors spread out so you can see each color by itself.

A specially-shaped piece of glass called a prism will also make white light spread out into the colors of the rainbow.

Use a water prism to make your own rainbow.

1 Fill a tank or a bowl with water.

2 Put the tank in front of a white surface.

3 Hold a mirror in the water at an angle. You need to make a triangular-shaped piece of water that will work like a prism.

4 Wait until the water has settled and the surface is flat.

5 Gently move the mirror until you see a rainbow appear on the white surface.

6 Then fix the mirror in place with corks or modeling clay.

7 Draw a picture of the colors in your rainbow.

Another way to show that white light is made up of the colors of the rainbow is to make a color spinner.

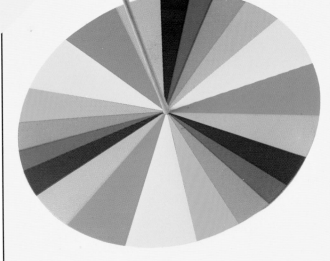

1 Cut out a circle of white cardboard.

2 Color the circle to match the one in the picture. Or divide the disk into six equal sections and color them in the main rainbow colors – red, orange, yellow, green, blue, and violet. Make sure the colors are in exactly this order.

3 Sharpen a pencil and push it through the middle of the circle.

4 Flick your fingers to make the circle spin fast, like a top.

5 The circle spins too fast for your eyes to see each color on its own. So the colors disappear and the circle looks yellowish-white.

Try making spinners with different mixtures of colors, like red and green, blue and red, or red and yellow. When you spin them, what colors do you see?

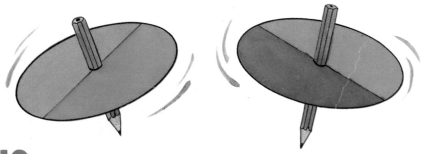

This photo was taken through a narrow set of openings called a diffraction grating. The grating has made the light spread out into the colors of the rainbow.

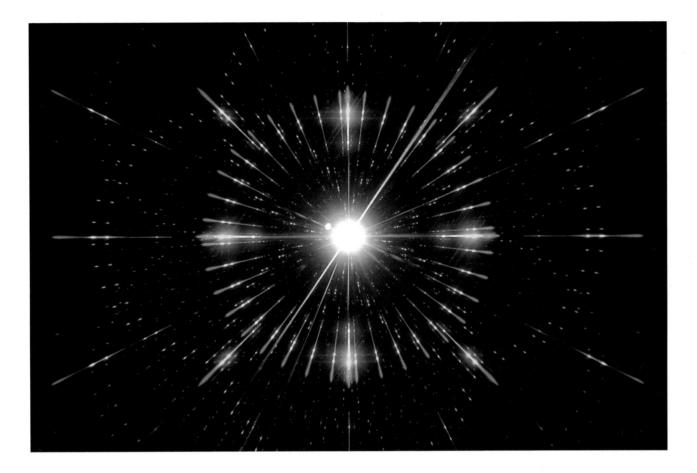

The light from a laser is very special. It is all one color and hardly spreads out at all. It cannot be split up into rainbow colors. The color of each laser depends on the material used to make the light inside the laser.

Laser lights are often used to create amazing effects at concerts. They can also cut holes in metal, repair damaged blood vessels, split diamonds, and read the prices on groceries in supermarkets.

SEEING COLORS

Have you ever wondered why grass looks green? When white light hits an object, some of the rainbow colors are taken in by the object. This is called absorption. The other colors bounce back from the object. This is called reflection. We see the colors that are reflected from objects into our eyes. Green grass or green paper reflect green light and absorb the other colors, so they look green.

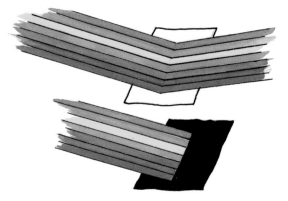

Why do some objects look black or white? If something absorbs all the rainbow colors, no colors are reflected and it looks black. If something reflects all the rainbow colors, it looks white.

In the same way, paints look different colors because of the colors they reflect. Green paint reflects green light. What color does red paint or blue paint reflect?

Try mixing colors with your paints. Can you make all the colors of the rainbow? How many different shades of red can you make? You can make most colors by mixing blue, yellow or red. These important colors are called the primary colors of paint. Together, they make dark brown.

yellow and blue
make green

red and blue
make purple

red and yellow
make orange

blue, red and yellow
make dark brown

Look at the pictures these children are holding. Which train stands out best against the background? The color of the background affects the way we see the colors of the objects near us.

Which colors are easiest to spot from a distance? Think about the colors of road signs. Which colors are used on warning signs?

Some people find it hard to tell the difference between certain colors. This is called color blindness. Many people who are color blind confuse reds and greens. This chart is a test for color blindness. People who are color blind confuse the pattern of dots and they cannot read the correct number.

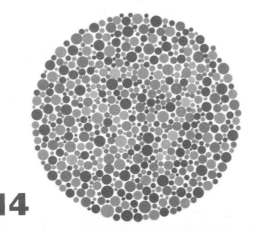

The way in which our eyes and brain "see" colors can sometimes cause our eyes to play tricks.

▶ Look at the plane with the orange nose. Is it nearer to the plane with the yellow nose or the one with the blue nose?

The plane with the yellow nose looks nearer, but if you measure the distances between the noses, you may be surprised at the result!

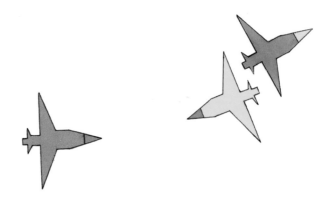

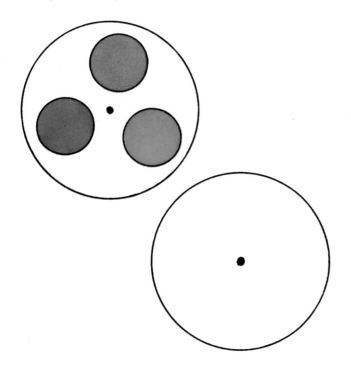

◀ Stare hard at the black dot between the colored circles for about 30 seconds. Now look over to the other black spot. What colors do you see?

When you stare hard at something, the nerves in your eyes that "see" each color get tired. So they stop "seeing" that particular color for a while. This is called nerve tiredness. When you look across at the other black dot, you should see green-blue (cyan) instead of red, and dark pink (magenta) instead of green. Which color do you see instead of blue?

◀ Stare at this cat. Look across at the window and you should see the cat. What color is it now?

Impressionist paintings such as this one by Seurat are made up of thousands of tiny dots. From a distance, the dots are too small to see and the pictures look as if they are made up of areas of flat color. To see how this works, try painting some dot pictures yourself. Use a thin brush and make sure the dots are very small and close together.

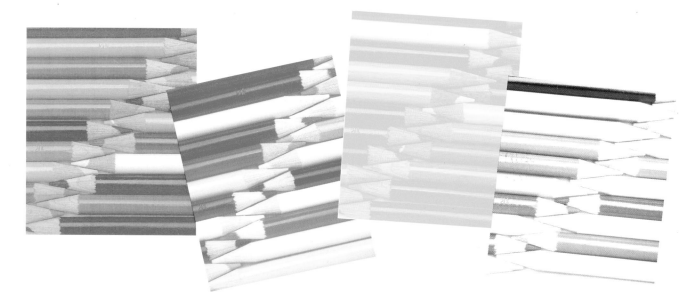

Before a painting or a photograph is printed in a book, it is separated into dots of four different colors – magenta, cyan, yellow and black.

out of register

Each one of the four colors is made into a separate printing plate. On the printing machine, ink is spread over the plates and the colors are printed one on top of the other. If the dots are not in exactly the right place, the picture looks fuzzy. This is called being "out of register."

CREEPING COLORS

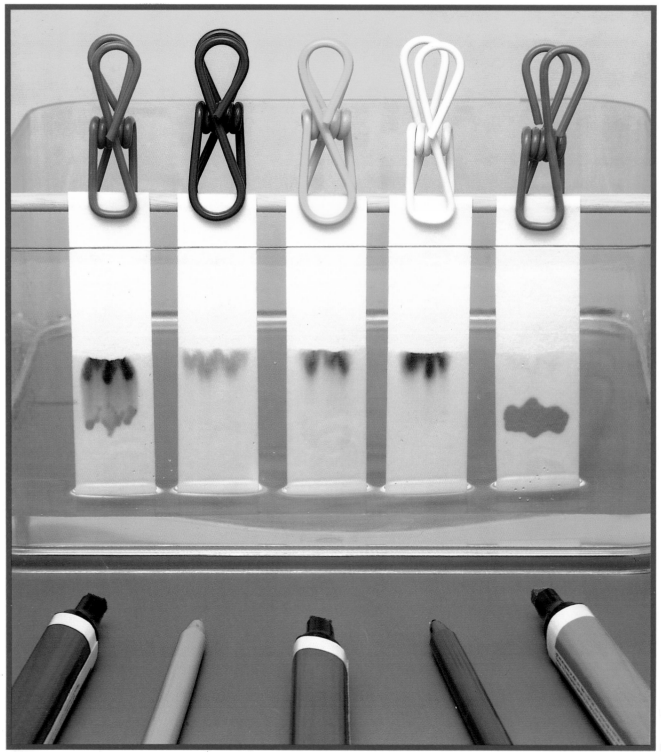

The inks in magic markers are often a mixture of different colored dyes. You can find out which dyes were used in each pen by chromatography, which means "color pictures." The police use chromatography to help them identify the pens used by forgers.

To see how chromatography works, try this test.

1 Cut some blotting paper or paper towel into thin strips. Make each strip about 1 inch wide and 8 inches long.

2 Choose several different magic markers to test.

3 Put a small blob of color about 1½ inches from the bottom of each strip of paper.

4 Fill a tank or bowl with about 1 inch of water.

5 Hang the strips above the tank so the end of each strip just dips into the water.

6 As the paper soaks up the water, the colors in each pen will creep up the strip. Some colors creep faster and further than others so you will see separate bands of color.

7 Before you put each strip into the water, see if you can guess which colors will appear.

You can use chromatography to make some rainbow pies. Cut out a circle of blotting paper and use several different magic markers to draw a pattern on the paper. Fold the paper in half and then in half again. Dip the folded point into some water and watch the colors explode! Carefully open out your circle and leave it to dry.

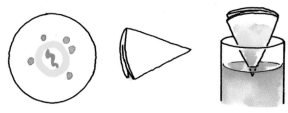

CHANGING COLOR

What does the world look like through rose-colored glasses? Try looking at objects through pieces of colored cellophane. Do the objects change color?

Have you even seen sunlight shining through a stained-glass window? The colored glass lets the light pass through. But each color lets only light of the same color pass through. It absorbs all the other colors. So the colored light that comes through the whole window is the same pattern of colors as the window itself.

Colored materials that allow light of the same color to pass though them are called filters.

In the photograph below, a red filter lets only red light through. The strawberry reflects red light so you can see the strawberry clearly with the light that has passed through the red filter. The white paper reflects all colors, but only red light gets through the filter, so the paper looks red.

The green filter lets only green light through. It absorbs the red light. Because there is no red light for the strawberry to reflect, it looks dark. Why does the paper look green through this filter?

COLORED LIGHT

You can use color filters to see what happens when you mix different colored lights. In the picture, you can see how a mixture of colored lights makes this boy and his clothes change color. All the colors were made by mixing red, green and blue light.

These important colors are called the primary colors of light.

**red and green light
make yellow light**

**red and blue light
make magenta light**

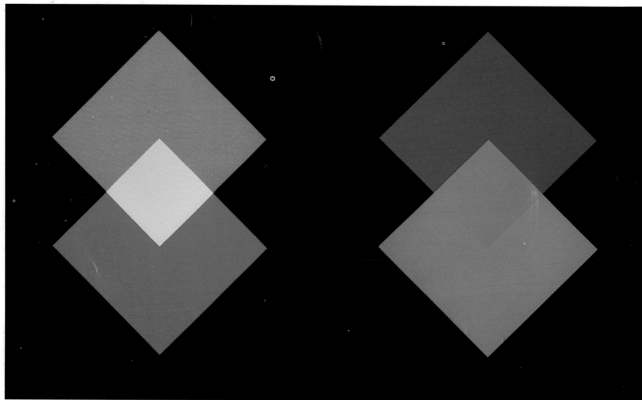

Colored lights are often used to give special effects at concerts and plays. Color filters are put in front of the lights to produce a different color.

Mixing light is not the same as mixing paints. Look back at page 13. How many differences can you find?

blue and green light make cyan light

red, blue and green light make white light

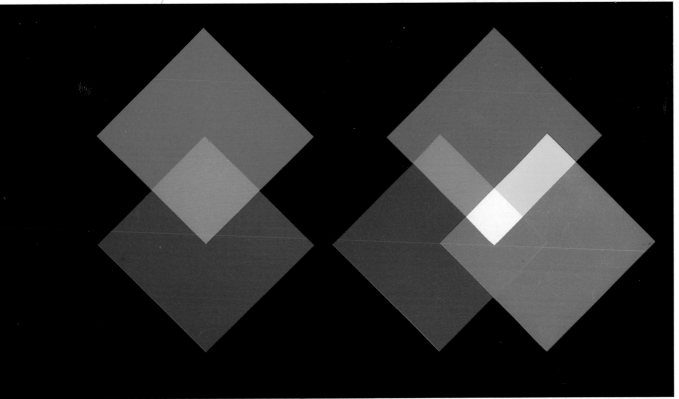

SKY COLORS

Do you know why the sky looks blue during the day and orange-red at sunrise and sunset?

To find out the answer, try this test.

1 Fill a glass with water.

2 Put about half a teaspoon of powdered cream for coffee into the water.

3 Let the powder sink down through the water – don't stir it.

4 Shine a flashlight onto the glass from above. The water should look a bluish color.

5 Now shine a flashlight through the glass from behind. What color does the water look now?

The grains of powdered cream scatter the light from the flashlight. When you shine the light from behind the glass, the blue light is scattered aside and only the orange-red light reaches your eyes. When the flashlight is above the glass, less light is scattered and more blue light reaches your eyes. So the water looks blue.

The same thing happens to the sunlight in the sky, where the dust and gases do the scattering. The colors in the sunlight are scattered by different amounts according to the position of the sun in the sky.

BUBBLES...

Have you ever blown a giant bubble?
Can you see the rainbow colors in this bubble? Are big bubbles different colors from small bubbles? To make your bubbles last longer, add some glycerine to the bubble mix.

26

...SHELLS AND PUDDLES

Where do the colors come from? The bubble mix has no color of its own and the colors are not spread out as they are in a prism. Instead, the colors are formed when white light is reflected from the outer and inner surfaces of the bubble. This is called interference. For each color, the reflections can add up so we see that color very brightly. Or they can cancel each other out so we see a dark area.

You can also see interference colors inside some shells. The colors are reflected from the thin layers of pearly materials that make up the shell.

A thin layer of oil lying on a surface will also produce interference colors. Look out for these colors on roads and puddles. How do the colors change if you look at them from different angles?

Feather rainbows

The rows of slits in a feather work like a diffraction grating to split up white light into the colors of the rainbow.

Ask an adult to light a candle for you. Make sure the candle is in a safe holder so it won't tip over. Stand about 12 inches away from the candle, shut one eye and look through the outer edge of the feather. Can you see patches of rainbow colors? What happens to the colors if you turn the feather around? (Don't forget to blow out the candle when you have finished.)

Making rainbows

You can use a garden hose to make your own rainbow. Do this in the early morning or late afternoon when the sun is low in the sky. Stand with your back to the sun and spray a fine shower of water from the hose. A circular rainbow will appear in the spray. If you look at the rainbow against a dark background, like a fence or a tree, you will be able to see it more clearly.

Choosing colors

What is your favorite color? Make a survey of the favorite colors of your friends. Which are the most popular colors? Which colors go well together? Do people choose to wear different colored clothes depending on the weather, their mood or for some other reason? You could try sorting colors into groups like summer and winter colors, happy and sad colors, hot and cold colors, or nice and nasty colors.

Make some color glasses

Cut out the frames of a pair of glasses from a piece of cardboard. Leave a hole for each eye piece. Stick a piece of colored cellophane over each eye piece. Put on the glasses and look at things indoors and out of doors. Make a list of the colors things seem to be through the glasses. Then take off the glasses and see what colors things really are.

What happens if you put red cellophane over one eye and green cellophane over the other eye?

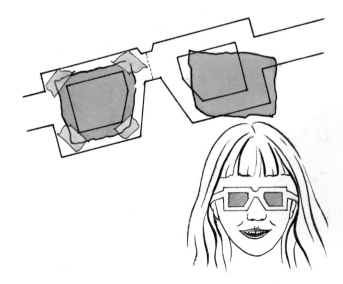

Colors at night

Which colors show up best in the dark? Cut out a circle of cardboard and paint some blobs of different colors on it. Put the cardboard in the bottom of a box with a lid. Make a viewing hole in the top of the box and several small holes in one side.

Cover all the holes on the side of the box except one. Look through the viewing hole. Which colors show up best when there is very little light inside the box? To gradually let more light into the box, uncover the holes in the side one at a time. Which colors show up best in the light?

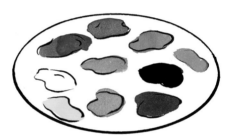

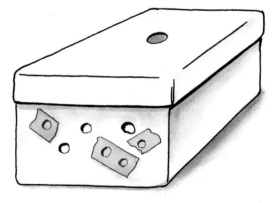

Collecting colors

Make a collection of objects that are all the same color. Choose some natural materials like stones, leaves or flowers and some manmade materials like plastic, paper or metal. How many shades of the same color can you find?

Spotting colors

Draw several outline shapes of an insect like a bee or a ladybug. Cut out the shapes and color each one differently. Make some shapes a solid color and others a pattern of spots or stripes.

Now hide your insects on leaves and branches in the garden or the playground. How many of the insects can your friends find in three minutes? Which insects are easiest to find? See if you can find out the names of some real insects with spots or stripes. You could design camouflage patterns for different backgrounds.

Tie-dyeing

Try tie-dyeing some cloth with artificial dyes or dyes made from plants like beets, onion or spinach. To make the plant dyes, put the plant material into an old bowl and ask an adult to pour boiling water on top. Leave the bowl to stand for a few hours and strain off the colored liquid.

Then put an object such as a small stone on the cloth and use cotton or string to tie the cloth around the object. When you dip the cloth in the dye, the tie stops the color reaching some parts of the cloth, which makes interesting patterns. To make a variety of patterns, tie the cloth several times, or knot the cloth itself.

▲ In one human eye, there are about seven million cells that respond to color. Because of their shape, these cells are called cones. They need bright light to work well and help us to see in the daytime. There are three types of cone and each type is sensitive to one of the primary colors, red, green or blue.

Birds have five types of cone cell, so they can tell the difference between colors we see as the same.

▲ Color blindness is inherited so it tends to run in families. It is also linked to the genes that control the development of a baby into a boy rather than a girl. This means that more males are color blind than females. About eight in every one hundred males and about one in every one hundred females have some form of color blindness. Very few people suffer from true color blindness, which is when a person sees only in black, white and gray. This affects about one in every 40,000 people.

▲ Many animals, such as the peacock, use colors to show off and help them to attract a mate. Female birds are often dull colors. This helps to camouflage them from enemies when they are sitting on their eggs.

▲ The color of a bird's eggs often keeps them camouflaged. However, an owl's eggs are glossy white, which means the owl can see them at night.

▲ The picture on a television screen is made up of changing patterns of tiny red, blue and green dots, which are very close together. Our eyes cannot see the individual dots and the brain "sees" areas of smooth, flat color.

▲ Albert Einstein worked out the theory of the laser in 1917, but the first laser was not made until 1960 by an American scientist, Theodore H. Maiman.

▲ Strips of transparent black and white film for cameras were first brought out in 1888. In color photography Kodachrome film was introduced in 1936 in America. It was available before the Second World War, but was only in limited use. It was only really in the 1950s that cameras were designed to take color film.

▲ People have made up different sayings to help them remember the order of colors in a rainbow. For example: "Roy G BIV."

▲ People have invented lots of different sayings that use colors. For example: as red as a beet; as good as gold; as green as grass; once in a blue moon. Do you know what these sayings mean: "feeling off color," "to come off with flying colors," "to see red?"

▲ In Hinduism and Buddhism saffron is a color of holiness and some Buddhist monks can be seen wearing saffron robes.

▲ In Southeast Asia, China and Japan red is a color of good fortune. White is worn at Buddhist and Hindu funerals.

▲ The Hindu festival of Holi in early March celebrates the return of color and warmth to the land. People throw colored powder (gulal) or squirt colored water over each other.

▲ In the Middle East many of the mosaics in the mosques are in cool colors – greens and blues – to signify that they are places of refreshment.

Camouflage
A coloring or pattern that matches the background and makes things hard to see. Some animals, soldiers, tanks, guns, ships and airplanes are camouflaged.

Chromatography
A way of separating mixtures of gases, liquids or dissolved substances.

Color blindness
Being unable to tell the difference between certain colors, such as red and green.

Cyan
A green-blue color.

Diffraction of light
The effect caused by passing light through a row of narrow openings. This splits up the light into the colors of the spectrum.

Dyes
Chemical substances that are used to color cloth and other materials.

Filter
A screen that stops things passing through it. A color filter lets through light of the same color as the filter. It stops any other colors.

Interference of light
The formation of bright colors or light and dark bands as a result of the reflections of a particular color adding together or canceling each other out.

Laser
A device that produces a narrow, very powerful beam of light of one color which travels over long distances without spreading out. Laser stands for **L**ight **A**mplification by **S**timulated **E**mission of **R**adiation.

Magenta
A dark pink color.

Primary color
One of the three colors of paint or light that can be mixed to make any other color. The primary colors of light are red, green and blue. The primary colors of paint are red, yellow and blue.

Prism
A solid shape made of glass or another transparent material, which has equal and parallel ends (often triangular) and sides with parallel edges.

Reflection
The bouncing back of rays of light from a surface.

Spectrum
The band of colors that makes up white light. These are the colors we see in a rainbow – red, orange, yellow, green, blue, indigo and violet.

White light
Light from the sun or an artificial source, such as an electric light bulb, which looks white but is in fact made up of the colors of the spectrum.

INDEX

absorption 12
angles 9, 27
animals 5, 6, 7

birds 5, 6, 30
brain 15
bubbles 26, 27

camouflage 6, 29, 30, 31
chameleon 6
chromatography 19, 31
clothes 7, 28
color blindness 14, 30, 31
color messages 4, 5
color pictures 19
color spinner 10
color tricks 15
cone cell 30
cyan 15, 17, 23, 31

diffraction 31
diffraction grating 11, 28
dots 16, 17
dyes 19, 29, 31

Einstein, Albert 30
electric light 8, 31
emergency vehicles 7
eyes 12, 15, 30

filters 21, 22, 23, 31

genes 30
glass 9, 30
glasses 20, 28

hearing 5

inks 17, 19
interference colors 28, 31

lasers 11, 30, 31

magenta 15, 17, 22, 31
Maiman, Theodore H. 30
mirror 9
mixing colors 10, 12, 13, 19

nerves 15

oil 27

painting 16, 17
paints 12, 23, 31
photography 17, 30
primary colors 12, 13, 22, 27, 30, 31
printing 17
prism 9

rainbows 8, 9, 10, 11, 12, 19, 26, 28, 30, 31
raindrops 8
reflected light 28
reflections 12, 27, 31
register 17
religion 30
religious festivals 30

safety clothes 7
scattered light 24
senses 5
Seurat 16
shells 27
sky 8, 24, 25
smell 5
soccer teams 4
special effects 23
spectrum 8, 31
stained-glass 20
sun 8, 25, 28, 31
sunlight 8, 25
sunrise 24
sunset 24
surface 9

television 4, 30
traffic lights 4
transparent 31

warning colors 7, 14
water 9, 24, 28
water prism 9
white light 8, 9, 10, 12, 27, 28, 31

Additional photographs:
Heather Angel/Biofotos 6 (t), 7 (t);
Chapel Studios 23 (t); Courtauld
Institute Galleries, London
(Courtauld Collection) 16 (t);
Chris Fairclough: 4; CFCL/Tony
Zirkel 24 (r); CFCL/Paul Blowfield
25 (t); Rex Features: 3 (tl), 8, 11 (b);
Trustees of the Science Museum,
London/David Exton (Launch
Pad) 22 (t); Science Photo Library:
11 (t).
**Picture researcher:
Sarah Ridley**